24 SEVEN FAITH

Dr. Bracken Christian

TABLE OF CONTENTS

ক্ষ

ISBN _978-0-578-68555-7
Printed in the United States of America

INTRODUCTION

᪥

Faith excites God like nothing else! Jesus asked, "When the Son of Man comes, will He find faith on the earth?" (Luke 18:8). It is recorded, "Men of old gained approval by faith" (Hebrews 11:39).

Many people might not like the term 'pleasing to God,' but we cannot please God without faith, "Without faith it is impossible to please God" (Hebrews11:6). The Apostle Paul instructed us "Walk as children of Light" (Ephesians 5:8). Verse 10 continues, "trying to learn what is pleasing to the Lord." God loves all men because He is love. But when you please Him, favor will flow and the impossible will be made possible.

Faith can walk on water, move mountains, heal sickness, open blind eyes, break chains, raise the dead, receive answered prayer, change circumstances, do the impossible, and receive miracles. Someone has said, "Faith is living in the midst of a miracle, on the edge of disaster."

Walking by faith and not by sight is easier said than done (see 2 Cor. 5:7). **Faith requires unquestioning trust in God's word over natural circumstances.** The greatest example of this is demonstrated in the life of Abraham. Abraham's example of obedience is worthy of study, especially since he is referred to in the Scriptures as the 'Father of Faith.'

Abraham's life of faith and obedience began with a call from God 'to go' when he did not know where he was going, and to receive a promise that would make him the 'Father of Many Nations.' His faith became unshakeable in the midst of natural circumstances that boldly proclaimed, "Impossible"! Yet today, it is sad to say, too many go into shock over a roadblock in life. That is why we must understand that **faith makes the impossible, possible!**

Abrahams faith was so great that while he lived in the land of promise, he still maintained his focus on the "city which has foundations, whose architect and builder is God" (Hebrews 11:9-10). We are called to live life by the same design. We are to trust God in the valleys, wildernesses, the unknown and through any and all trials.

Faith has been communicated by many in different ways because it can be used in every aspect or arena of life. It is required for prayer, giving, receiving finances or healing. It is required for resisting the enemy and overcoming in life. Paul urged Timothy to "Fight the good fight of faith" (1 Timothy 6:12).

Most of the miracles that happened in Jesus' ministry were received or activated by faith. Over and over, Jesus made reference to someone's faith making them whole. In approximately 80% of cases of healing or miracles, He performed healing and miracles using the term 'your faith made you well;' (e.g. Luke 17:19).

The Christian life is to be lived by faith. It is a command, not an option. Paul sums it up:

> I have been crucified with Christ; and it is no longer I who live, but Christ who lives in me; and the life which I now live in the flesh I live by faith in the Son of God, who loved me and gave Himself up for me. (Galatians 2:20)

The author of Hebrews reminds us of an Old Testament scripture; "But My righteous one shall live by faith (Habakkuk 2:4), And if he shrinks back, My soul has no pleasure in him" (Hebrews 10:38). Notice the statement "live by faith" and again the emphasis on God's pleasure when we live by faith.

Living by faith is a 24 hours-a-day, 7 days-a-week responsibility! Faith, though it works the same in every area, must be developed in every area. It begins with God's gift; "God has given to every man the measure of faith (Romans 12:3). What a man begins to do with that 'measure' determines what he does and has in life. **Progress in this Christian life only takes place by faith**.

Faith is for 'now' in this life. It is one of the 'big three' that Paul emphasizes; "But Now faith, hope, love, abide these three; but the greatest of these is love" (1 Corinthians 13:13). Faith helps get you through the 'now of life' as you believe God, but it also pulls you through to 'the eternal' as we, like Abraham, look for the city whose builder and maker is God.

Faith is about expecting something good because we are persuaded of something true.

We must imitate Abraham who was fully persuaded that God was able to do what he promised (Romans 4:21). If we are not persuaded then we will settle for less. We are to become fully persuaded not only of the promises God has offered in His word for us now, but also of things to come, i.e.; the return of Jesus, the Millennial Reign of Christ, the new heavens and the new earth.

While He hears us, God is not moved to action by needs or crying. He responds to our faith. In fact, *God requires our faith.*

FAITH IS A FIRM PERSUASION

We must keep the faith, unwavering in our conviction. The Apostle Paul made an amazing statement concerning Gods call on his life and ministry near the end of his life, "I have fought the good fight, I have finished the course, I have kept the faith" (2 Tim 4:7).

Let's please God in all our moments by trusting Him, but let's also please him by finishing our course, and hearing him say, "Well done good and faithful servant...enter into the joy of your Master" (Matt. 25:23).

A person will have in this life what they believe for from God, nothing more and nothing less. Faith is the ingredient for everything and anything you will ever want to experience.

The reason that I wrote this book is to inspire that God kind of faith.

Faith Makes the Impossible, Possible!

Faith is my confident expectation—a firm foundation.

Living by faith is a 24 hours-a-day, 7 days-a-week responsibility!

Progress in this Christian life only takes place by faith.

ഇ 1 രെ

FAITH IS BASED ON KNOWLEDGE OF THE REVEALED WILL OF GOD

~~~~~

Faith is seeing and living in the unseen realm, knowing the visible world is temporal. "We look not at the things that are seen, which are temporal, but at the unseen" (2 Cor. 4:18). It takes faith for us to speak to temporal circumstances which can be changed by our words. A powerful man of God said,

Any man can be changed by faith, no matter how he may be fettered. I know that God's word is sufficient. One word from him can change a nation. (Smith Wigglesworth, Internet quote)

Reinhard Bonnke was a German-American Pentecostal evangelist, known for his crusades throughout Africa. When the main speaker did not show up for Bonnke's first crusade, the Lord told him to do the meeting saying, "My words in your mouth are as powerful as My words in My mouth."

When Bonnke looked at the crowd, the circumstances could have looked overwhelming. Surely, he felt fear at being adequate for the task. But we live by believing and not by seeing (see 2 Cor. 5:7).

This example of Bonke's first crusade can be applied to all of our situations. We need to be saying what God says! That is living by faith and having the God kind of faith. Jesus helped Brother Hagin understand Mark 11:22-23 by explaining that people must do three times the saying as they do believing:

> "Have faith in God," Jesus answered. "Truly I tell you, if anyone says to this mountain, 'Go, throw yourself into the sea,' and does not doubt in their heart but believes that what they say will happen, it will be done for

them. Therefore I tell you, whatever you ask for in prayer, believe that you have received it, and it will be yours. And when you stand praying, if you hold anything against anyone, forgive them, so that your Father in heaven may forgive you your sins." (Mark 11:22-26)

Another whose words ring true today said, "Faith is the opposite of sight" (Andrew Murray-Internet quote). That would bring to mind—two ways you can live, by faith or by mere sight.

Even if, as with the Psalmist, you must go through 'the valley of the shadow of death,' then you don't beg, and you don't fear, for you 'know' God is with you! (See Psalm 23). Look to His Word—His will.

FAITH IS BASED ON KNOWLEDGE OF THE REVEALED WILL OF GOD!

When you were a child trying to get something from your parents. Why did you repeatedly beg them for it? It is because you were not sure they would do it. That is the opposite of faith. Faith believes that if and when you ask, you have received. You may not see it but you believe you have it. **Faith always has a knowing to it, a substance**.

Remind yourself constantly that God's Word is His will! We agree that salvation is God's will, but know that everything that goes with salvation is His will, such as healing, provision, protection, safety. It is all God's will—as contained in His word.

Most of the world is in darkness and does not know God's will (His Word). Many are like the leper who came to Jesus for healing, but was not sure if He would heal him.   He did not know His will:

> A leper came to Him and bowed down before Him, and said, "Lord, if You are willing, You can make me clean." Jesus stretched out His hand and touched him, saying, "I am willing; be cleansed." And immediately his leprosy was cleansed. (Matthew 8:2-3)

GOD WANTS HIS PEOPLE TO KNOW HIS WILL

God loves the world, so he sent his Son to accomplish redemption, which was the will of God. Jesus knew the importance of knowing God's will, and said, "I did not come to do my own will, but the will of Him who sent me" (John 6:38). His will is for all to be saved. The Apostle Peter makes this clear,

> The Lord is not slack concerning His promise, as some count slackness, but is longsuffering toward us, not willing that any should perish but that all should come to repentance. (2 Peter 3:9)

God's will is a manifestation of His nature. God is love, life, goodness, peace, joy, generosity, and righteous. **Our perception of Him has a major impact on what and how we receive from Him**.

We can only discover God's will from His Word. **You cannot separate God's Word from Him or from His will**. Jesus Christ, our Lord, is the Word of God. The first sentence in the gospel of John makes this clear:

> In the beginning was the Word, and the Word was with God, and the Word was God. (John 1:1)

The book of Revelation gives us His name:

> He is clothed with a robe dipped in blood, and His name is called The Word of God. (Revelation 19:13))

Jesus describes His own words as "spirit and life" (John 6:63). The Word is also truth, as He is the Truth, the Amen (see John 8:31-32, 17:17). And All His promises are Yes and Amen (See 2 Cor. 1:20):

> Because he who is blessed in the earth Will be blessed by the God of truth; And he who swears in the earth Will swear by the God of truth. (Isaiah 65:16)

Truth cannot be a lie and cannot lie:

> God is not a man, that He should lie, Nor a son of man, that He should

repent; Has He said, and will He not do it? Or has He spoken, and will He not make it good? (Numbers 23:19) **It is impossible for God to lie**. (Hebrews 6:18)

God's DNA – His very life is in his word—it is the seed of Divine Life (1 Peter 1:23). The Word we read and speak carries the same authority as if the Master stood in our room and spoke it to us!

God does nothing apart from his Word. The Psalmist tell us, "For You have magnified Your word above all Your name" (Psalm 138:2). The word is enduring, "Forever, O Lord, Your word is settled in heaven" (Psalm 119:89).

Even the angels respond to His Word:

Bless the LORD, you His angels, mighty in strength, who perform His word, obeying the voice of his word! (Psalm 103:20)

The word of the Lord from Isaiah tells us that God's word is like rain coming down to water the earth:

> For as the heavens are higher than the earth, So are My ways higher than your ways And My thoughts than your thoughts. "For as the rain and the snow come down from heaven, And do not return there without watering the earth And making it bear and sprout, And furnishing seed to the sower and bread to the eater; So will My word be which goes forth from My mouth; It will not return to Me empty, Without accomplishing what I desire, And without succeeding in the matter for which I sent it. (Isaiah 55:9-11)

God's word is also like seed! It will produce a harvest.

> For you have been born again not of seed which is perishable but imperishable, that is, through the living and enduring word of God. But the word of the Lord endures forever." And

this is the word which was preached to you. (1 Peter 1:23, 24)

We plant the seed and water it to make it grow. As we begin to hunger for the Word more and more, God is able to bring us revelation of His will and our destiny. Peter encourages us;

Like newborn babies, long for the pure milk of the word, so that by it you may grow in respect to salvation. (1 Peter 2:2)

Without planting seed, you cannot expect a harvest. In the 'parable of the sower' Jesus taught that the seed, which is the Word going into good ground will produce thirty, sixty and or one hundred-fold depending on the soil—the heart (see Mark 4, Luke 8).

Our adversary, the Devil, has challenged God's Word from the beginning. His goal has been to create doubt. He challenged Eve in the beginning concerning what God had said about the Tree of the Knowledge of Good and Evil; "Has God said..." (Gen. 3:1).

When the devil came to tempt Jesus in the wilderness, he attacked God's Word in the process. Jesus always answered with the Word in three examples with "It is written."

In the Devil's first temptation, Jesus made it clear that we live by the Word of God.

> But He answered and said, "It is written, 'Man shall not live on bread alone, but on every word that proceeds out of the mouth of God.'" (Matthew 4:4)

The Bible is about God and His plan for man. It is a book of promises. And His promises are magnificent. Writes Peter,

> Grace and peace be multiplied to you in the knowledge of God and of Jesus our Lord; seeing that His divine power has granted to us everything pertaining to life and godliness, through the true knowledge of Him who called us by His own glory and excellence. 4 For by these He has granted to us His precious and magnificent promises, so that by them you may become partakers of the divine nature, having escaped the corruption

that is in the world by lust. (2 Peter 1:2-4)

IT IS IMPOSSIBLE FOR GOD'S WORD TO FAIL

If we continue in the Word, we will see that God "watches over His Word to perform it" (see Jeremiah 1). Therefore it will not fail. Israel would say without hesitation, God performed His promises:

> Blessed be the Lord, who has given rest to His people Israel, according to all that He promised; not one word has failed of all His good promise, which He promised through Moses His servant. (1 Kings 8:56)

Since the Son of God came and overcame the world, we see much of God's Word has been fulfilled. Jesus is our amen, the fulfilment of God's promise:

> For as many as are the promises of God, in Him they are yes; therefore also through Him is our Amen to the glory of God through us. (2 Corinthians 1:20)

THE WORD OF GOD IS THE FACTORY FOR FAITH!

All of the Bible is not about the subject of faith, but it has the capacity to produce faith in whatever area you need it. God's Word is to be our faith food. A prayer in faith can produce marvelous results. The beloved Apostle John writes,

> This is the confidence which we have before Him, that, **if we ask anything according to His will, He hears us**. And if we know that He hears us in whatever we ask, we know that **we have the requests** which we have asked from Him. (1 John 5:14-15)

Faith marked our beginning with God, because faith is a spiritual substance that is made available when we hear the Word of Truth. The Apostle Paul was a Hebrew scholar who knew the Old Testament very well. He urged his son in the faith, Timothy, to apply his life to that Word:

Be diligent to present yourself approved to God as a workman who does not need to be ashamed, accurately handling the word of truth. (2 Timothy 2:15)

Paul, quoting from Isaiah 53, asked the same question as Isaiah; "Lord, who has believed our message?" (Romans 10:16). The arm or (the power) of God is manifested (revealed) to those who believe the report.

The 'report' or 'message,' depending on the translation, is called 'the good news' for a reason. It is the good news of redemption, and what God has done for us in Christ.

Subsequently Paul then follows the question with the answer of how belief is established, and how faith comes; "Faith comes by hearing and hearing by the word of Christ" (Romans 10:17).

God's Word was written to reveal to us what He has done, what He desires for us, and what He wills to do for us, His very children. **We are to take His word and declare it— proclaim it**.

That is what Paul meant when he said:

> For I am not ashamed of the gospel, for it is the power of God for salvation to everyone who believes, to the Jew first and also to the Greek. For in it the righteousness of God is revealed from faith to faith; as it is written, "But the righteous man shall live by faith." (Romans 1:16-17)

While I was doing youth ministry in a church in Wheeler, Texas during the summer of 1990, I was asked to preach at a combined service out on a ranch. I was determined to get a 'word from heaven' and went on a three day fast several weeks before the meeting. During my time of fasting, I was spending extra time in the church auditorium seeking the Lord for the word in due season. To my surprise, He gave me a word, but the word was for me. I was reading and focusing on the first chapter of Joshua, where three times the Lord instructed Joshua to *"Be strong and of good courage."* I must have not been paying close enough attention to Him, because as I was praying in the auditorium one afternoon, the Holy Spirit powerfully yelled at me, "That's for you!"

One and one-half months after hearing from the Lord, my wife and I, along with our two small children, left for bible school with nothing but a few dollars and the confidence that moving to Oklahoma was God's next step for our lives. It was a challenging twenty-two months as we believed God with every ounce of faith that we had. When difficult times were regularly upon us, I would get in prayer and seek the Lord for encouragement and help. All that I would hear very clearly down on the inside was, *"Be strong and of good courage."* Even though I wanted to hear something else, that word was like an anchor in my heart, and it gave me courage to stand strong. A word from God will do that for any man who holds it fast.

GOD'S COMMANDS ARE ENABLING

The Bible gives us an account of a life changing moment for a woman who had experienced a hemorrhage of blood for twelve years. But her defining moment came when she heard about Jesus. Hearing about Him revealed God's plan for her.

> After hearing about Jesus, she came up in the crowd behind him and touched his cloak. For she said, "if I just touch his garments, I will get well." Immediately the flow of her blood was dried up; and she felt in her body that she was healed of her affliction. (Mark 5:27-29)

Jesus told her, "Daughter, your faith has made you well; go in peace and be healed of your affliction" (Mark 5:34).

Notice what she 'heard' gave her faith to obtain God's will for her life. Her faith took hold, and she would not be denied. Faith will make you do the impossible, and not take no for an answer. One interpretation of Hebrews 11 begins every example of faith with "His faith made him..." When the disciples saw Jesus coming to them on the water, the Lord's word to Peter encouraged him to do the same. Jesus came walking on the water and the disciples were startled. After recognizing it was Jesus, Peter said, "Lord if it is you command me to come." Jesus said, "Come." Peter acted on that word, got out of the boat, and walked on the water. (see Matthew 14)

If you want to walk on waters of the supernatural, then you must learn to stand on the promises of God's Word.

Faith always has a knowing to it!

The word of God is the factory for faith!

God's commands are enabling

Faith comes by hearing...

‰ 2 ‰

THE FRUIT OF FELLOWSHIP

~~~~~

A man that I much admire because of his wisdom and prayer life said, "God's greatest pain is to be doubted. His greatest pleasure is to be believed" (Mike Murdock).

I believe strongly that 'Faith thrives in the rich fertile soil of fellowship with God.' Time spent in God's Presence will aid in building a strong relationship. It takes faith to discipline one's self to seek God's Presence, but we must be intent on pleasing Him:

> Without faith it is impossible to please Him, for he who comes to God must believe that He is and that He is a rewarder of those who seek Him. (Hebrews 11:6)

An alternate translation of this verse shows us the ultimate reason for seeking God, His revelation of Himself. And that in itself is a great reward:

> Nobody reaches God's presence until he has learned to believe, until he has learned to believe that God exists and that He reveals himself to those who sincerely look for Him. (Hebrews 11:6, Knox and Taylor)

Man does not discover God, **God reveals himself to man**. And faith is the vehicle that draws God's attention. Never forget, the greatest honor, the greatest experience that a human being can have is to get to know God. It brings eternal life:

> This is eternal life, that they may know You, the only true God, and Jesus Christ whom You have sent. (John 17:3)

Real faith is the result of a living relationship and fellowship with God. Faith is not just based on what God said but the reliability of the One who said it.

Most people when they think of faith, think of a moment or moments in time. Many try and explain faith, and they start with Hebrews 11:1, "Now faith is." But the writer of Hebrews actually begins to set up the subject of faith from the previous chapter by explaining the importance of 'living' by faith, not a moment of faith (see Hebrews 10:32). Remember that the Bible was not written in chapter and verse, so when reading and studying, it is wise to look at the whole context.

Faith is never judged by a moment—It is judged over a lifetime. We want God to take pleasure in our faith.

> Now the just shall live by faith: but if any man draw back, my soul shall have no pleasure in him. (Hebrews 10:38)

Since most people think in terms of faith as a moment in time, they are frustrated because something didn't happen. And they get stuck in that particular moment. They feel like giving up because they are having to wait, but we can't view faith for a moment as in a microcosm, we must view it in terms of a broader scale. I have heard many say, "I believed and it didn't happen, so where's

God?" You probably have experienced that feeling before!

If we ever get consumed in the moment, then we will have the temptation to draw back. If we draw back, stop believing, and stop hoping, then God has no pleasure in us. We all have moments that make us question everything, including God. I learned a long time ago, learn to always stay on God's side.

Delay must always be challenged by confidence. Delay does not mean denial. Hebrews reminds us that our confidence will produce reward; "Don't cast away your confidence which has a great reward" (Hebrews 10:35). "....imitate those who through faith and patience inherit the promises" (Hebrews 6:12).

FEDERAL EXPRESS EXPERIENCE

God often helps us develop our faith during times of intense struggle. I would compare my years at Rhema Bible College as a struggle—while very fulfilling, our family had some very lean times! I would not trade those two years for anything. It was there that I truly learned to believe God for the smallest of things, and later for the greater things. My story of believing for a better job while there helps even now to keep the bigger perspective.

Working for minimum wage to support a family made me want to focus on a higher paying job at FedEx. I applied there and set my face to get the job. I went by there frequently to 'check-in' and keep my application fresh. Even my kids repeated that daddy was going to get on at FedEx. At meal time prayer, we thanked God for the job at FedEx. Then just before my class on the Holy Spirit one day, I heard, "You are going to get on at FedEx!" It was another five months before I finally got the call and immediately had to jump through some hoops to apply for a CDL License with a hazardous material requirement. I resigned my present job and went to work. However, the first day on the job, my boss called me in and apologized for letting me go. My driving record was not acceptable. It is rare that they hire someone without first checking their driving record, but I was so sure it was my job that he had hired me without checking. Can you imagine the devastation?

I summoned the courage to speak with my instructor at Rhema—Brother Keith Moore. When I told him my struggle—how my faith had been at work, he said four words, "Who is your source?" Well, I had to smile and go back to my minimum wage job. But the story doesn't end there. While working at that job I had met a man named, Lucius. Lucius had mentioned starting an alarm business, and had given me his card. Of course, at that time I had told him I was going to get on at FedEx, but I kept his card. As I was reading in class one day in Acts 13, I saw Lucius' name. It seemed to jump out at me. I followed up with Lucius, and I got a better job, one that allowed me to monitor security alarms my last six months at Rhema, and study and pray. It was both a financial opportunity and a study and prayer opportunity. From 5:00 PM until Midnight, I was in the Word and prayer. It is during that time that God gave me the vision for being a pastor—I had trained for youth ministry! Never under estimate God and His timing.

Before we ever understand the reality of faith, we must understand timing. Remember the importance of timing anytime faith is required. Faith is always looked at over a lifetime, never just a moment. If we will walk with God in faith over a lifetime, then there will be moments when we won't understand. We will look back and say, "It was worth walking in faith."

One might compare faith and timing to trying to cook based on a recipe. If the recipe calls for baking for twenty-five minutes but you take the food out of the oven after fifteen minutes, then it is the cook's fault if it didn't turn out as expected.

THREE WAYS SOME APPROACH FAITH:

1. Magic—you pull it out of a hat when life is bad and problems go away.

2. A formula—do these five, six or seven things or steps. A mechanical opportunity to 'try' to apply certain steps for a result.

3. Relationship—something that is built over a lifetime with God. Relationship is the main ingredient to meaningful faith.

THE GOD KIND OF FAITH

Having faith in God is easier when you are walking with God. Acting in faith can be much more difficult when you not walking with Him. Jesus taught that we must have faith in God, and as one translation puts it, the "God kind of faith;" "Have faith in God" (Mark 11:22).

If you are keeping a distance from God, then it is easier to have a magic wand or try six or seven steps to faith! When faith steps or formulas are emphasized without relationship, it is impossible to believe in God. A faith formula or steps can only work when you are walking with God.

The gospel of John has a story in Chapter 11 about Jesus raising His friend, Lazarus, from the dead. Jesus delayed two days in arriving—it would seem to make a point. When He arrives in Bethany, Mary and Martha, Lazarus' sisters take Jesus to the tomb. Jesus begins by praying, which was not what He normally did to perform a miracle;

> Father, I thank you that you have heard me. I knew that you always hear me, but I said this for the benefit of the people standing here, that they may believe that you sent me. Lazarus come forth. (John 11:41-43)

If you study what Jesus did, then it is impossible to come up with five steps or a formula or even magic. No, the fact is that Jesus was with His Father all the time, and He had a relationship that inspired His faith. This is exactly what Paul meant:

> I have been crucified with Christ; And it is no longer I who live, but Christ lives in me; And the life which I now live in the flesh I live by faith in the Son of God, who loved me and gave himself up for me. (Galatians 2:20)

This is a statement of relationship and mindset regarding Someone with whom we identify and have fellowship. It is true that the more you spend time with someone, the more opportunity you have to know them. The greatest secret of faith is Christ in me!

The Apostle Paul writing to Timothy said, "I know in whom I have believed…" (2 Timothy 1:12). Today many know 'about' God, but knowing someone and knowing about someone are two different things.

IT IS IN COMITTED RELATIONSHIPS THAT FAITH GROWS AND DEVELOPS.

Knowing God is inseparable from faith in him. Thus, you cannot have faith in God beyond the degree that you know Him.

It is possible to know scriptures and yet not know God. It is possible to know principles, steps, formulas and not know God. Faith is knowing God. Faith is a relationship with God.

The 'Faith Hall of Fame' contained in Hebrews 11 is actually about a list of Old Testament 'heroes of faith' who knew something about God to a certain degree.

Never think of the Bible apart from the Person—God. **A life of faith that echo's throughout eternity is a life that never lost its romance with God.**

IT IS IN THE ROMANCE THAT YOU DISCOVER HIS VOICE!

How precious is His voice! Had I not spent time worshipping Him, singing to Him, studying His Word and in fervent prayer, then I might not have ever heard His voice. It means so much to have fellowship—a conversation with One whom you love. It is in the rich fertile soil of fellowship that faith develops.

A faith life is a life that knows Him and fellowships with Him...

Faith is viewed over a lifetime...

We must have the right perspective...

You cannot have faith in God beyond the degree that you know Him...

Delay must always be challenged by confidence...

ಏ 3 ಐ

FAITH IS KNOWLEDGE AND VISION

~~~~~

God gives to each man a 'measure of faith,' but then it is up to the man to grow that faith. Knowledge of God and His Word is the major step that will begin to produce more faith. Much is packed into that sentence regarding knowledge of God; e.g., fellowship, fervent prayer, fasting, study of the Word with a view to not just produce a message but know the Writer. A well know radio news icon who covered daily stories of importance wrote:

A blind man's world is bound by the limits of his touch, an ignorant man's world by the limits of his knowledge, a great man's world by the limits of his vision. (Paul Harvey-Internet Quote)

THE CONNECTION BETWEEN FAITH AND VISION

God often gave His prophets visions—and often they acted out what He spoke to them to do in order to demonstrate what God was about to bring to pass. God required one such prophet to write what He spoke to Him:

> I will stand on my guard post and station myself on the rampart; And I will keep watch to see what He will speak to me, and how I may reply when I am reproved. Then the Lord answered me and said, "Record the vision and inscribe it on tablets, that the one who reads it may run. For the vision is yet for the appointed time; It hastens toward the goal and it will not fail. Though it tarries, wait for it; For it will certainly come, it will not delay." (Habakkuk 2:1)

What we hear produces mental sight. It does not matter if it is someone speaking or a song. The reason feelings or emotions are attached to what is heard or even thought is because they are connected to a picture!

The righteous are to live by vision--which is faith! The two are inseparable. Righteous believers must live by faith:

> Behold, as for the proud one, His soul is not right within him; But the righteous will live by his faith. (Habakkuk 2:4)

To capture the importance of this revelation is to once again look at the man who is called 'The Father of Faith,' Abraham. To instill in Abraham a vision for God's promise to Abraham of descendants, God showed him a picture:

> And He took him outside and said, "Now look toward the heavens, and count the stars, if you are able to count them." And He said to him, "So shall your descendants be." Then he believed in the Lord; and He reckoned it to him as righteousness. (Genesis 15:5-6)

Why is Abraham going to be called the Father of Faith? He is called the Father of Faith because Abraham believed God:
    "...Abraham "believed God, and it was

credited to him as righteousness." (see Genesis 12, Gal. 3:6, James 2:23, Romans 4:3)

To bring Abraham to that position of faith, God first gave him a vision. **The first thing God did was show him a picture of what could be**. That is faith's opportunity!

This is actually the second time God had spoken to Abraham about his descendants. The first time was when God told him, "his descendants would be as the dust of the earth" (Genesis 13:16).

Paul wrote to encourage the Corinthian Church about the spirit of faith—not focusing on the temporal, even a temporary life:

> While we look not at the things which are seen, but at the things which are not seen; for the things which are seen are temporal, but the things which are not seen are eternal. (2 Cor 4:18)

If we are ever going to learn how to look at the unseen, then we must understand that there are two kinds of vision, natural vision and spiritual vision. Webster's Dictionary describes vision as "not only the act of seeing but also the ability to see."

When it comes to spiritual vision, we have all been given the ability to see. That is faith's opportunity as the two are connected.

We need to understand the connection between faith and vision. Spiritual vision is seeing with the eyes of your heart. In one sense that is called faith. Paul writing to the Corinthian Church: "for we walk by faith not by sight" (2 Cor 5:7). The verse is talking about not walking by natural sight.

To walk by faith would mean to walk by 'spiritual vision.' That means to operate by spiritual sight, with the eyes of your heart. God's Word produces sight. We are to live from His words. Living words in the Bible produce vision. God speaks so you can go to a whole new level.

A major factor in our level of victory in life has to do with that to which we are looking, what we see, and then on what we set our focus.

Moses, for example, was a winner in life not because of what he saw, but because of who he saw:

> By faith he forsook Egypt, not fearing the wrath of the king: for he endured, as seeing him who is invisible. (Hebrews 11:27)

During certain times in life, it takes faith to walk away from something with which you have been comfortable, in order to choose the invisible over the visible. Moses found strength to do what he did, to stand up against the greatest empire in the world at that time, and declare, "Let my people go" (Exodus 9:1). He found strength to lead the Hebrews out of Egypt and through the Red Sea, the strength to walk with them for forty years, and he endured by "seeing Him Who is invisible."

If you do not have some type of vision (an inward realization), a mental image of a spiritual picture, a concept formed by the word of God illuminated in your heart, then you will not be able to endure. Because Without a spiritual picture (a vision for your future) you will not get out of Egypt, your past, or be able to stand the spiritual pressures of life.

Moses won because of what he saw. He walked in conquest because he saw someone who is invisible, not with the physical eyes but with spiritual eyes. It is important to understand that you have spiritual eyes. Writes Job, "I have heard of You by the hearing of the ear; But now my eye sees You" (Job 42:5). Job is referring to personal revelation, a vision of God after the Devil had stolen from him. And importantly, without personal revelation the devil can steal from you.

We are never wise to base our life on everything we see with our natural eyes, because those things change. However, certain things never change. God does not change. Whatever He says is forever, because it is "established in heaven" (Psalm 119:89).

We have a God who changes not, a Word that changes not, and a redemption that changes not. That is on what we should keep our eye's

toward. That is on what we should focus—
the unseen. Remember, "Now faith is the
substance of things hoped for, the evidence of
things not seen" (Hebrews 11:1). Therefore,
faith is the substance of unseen realities.

FAITH AND VISION ARE INSEPARABLE

King Solomon's wisdom from the Proverbs
states it clearly; "Without a vision (spiritual
sight) people perish" (Proverbs 29:18 my
addition). You can go down, down, down,
with natural sight. If this verse was talking
about natural vision, then everyone who had
good eyes would have victory and not perish.
Solomon is talking about a vision of another
kind—the kind of seeing that is directly
connected and linked up with faith.

Faith is Accompanied by Spiritual Sight

To walk by faith is to walk by spiritual sight,
and if you are going to operate in faith, you
must see.

You may be thinking, "See what?" You need

to see what God has said in general and specifically for your own faith life.

Make note again that "faith comes by hearing." Now put the two together. When you hear, what does that produce? Faith, yes, but it also produces sight.

In other words, you don't just hear it, you see it. Both are involved in faith. Never forget that when it comes to faith, you need to see it. My personal faith is stronger today than in the past; why? I see more! And I can tell you that there is a lot more to see. Aristotle, a Greek philosopher, wrote, "The soul never thinks without a picture."

As a pastor I like to communicate effectively because it can be the difference between success and failure for people. If they do not see anything when I am preaching, then I did not do any good—we did not communicate properly.

Words are merely vehicles that we use to paint pictures. A good story teller uses words well. He takes words and paints a picture on a canvas for you. Every word is another stroke of the brush. Were I to say, red convertible BMW, or black shaggy dog, you get a mental picture. You can write those words down. type them up, look and analyze them, but those words mean nothing unless you can begin to see.

Why has God given us His Word? Because He wants to put His vision in us. It is vision of victory, life, health, and peace. God knows what is in us will help guide us and lead us into victory. Keep in mind a winner's success who majored in faith can be followed:

Thinking faith thoughts, and speaking faith words, will lead the heart out of defeat and into victorty. (Kenneth E. Hagin, Internet Quote)

A life of faith that echo's throughout eternity is a life that never lost its romance with God...

Faith is accompanied with spiritual sight...

The soul never thinks without a picture...

Faith and vision are inseparable...

℘ 4 ℛ

OVERCOMING IN LIFE WILL REQUIRE AN ATTITUDE OF FAITH

≈≈≈≈

To be an overcomer in this life will require walking by faith. Faith is the main factor in any attempt to overcome life's hurdles. Lillian Yomen has written of this requirement:

> God has tied himself irrevocably to human cooperation in the execution of divine purpose. He has made man's faith a determining factor in the work of redemption. (Yomen, Lilian B., His Healing Power)

Our starting point was the fact that 'faith begins where the knowledge of the will of God is known.' **To find and to be in God's specific will for your life is to become**

invincible. When you know what God has done for you or instructed you to do, there's nothing left but to do it!

Faith is the substance that gives you the overcoming ability you need to overcome what 'comes' your way and receive what is yours.

Jesus' final words to all seven churches in the book of Revelation ends with "**to him who overcomes...**". Overcoming in life will require an attitude of faith. The faith-life is not a sprint but a marathon—one that you run all your life. It is faith that brings the victory. Writes the Apostle John,

> For whatsoever is born of God overcomes the world: and this is the victory that overcomes the world even our faith. (1 John 5:4)

Our faith makes us overcome because we believe in what God has done for us in Christ! The salvation that He won for us includes more than just missing hell. It means that we have victory through Jesus Christ in every area of life, because it has been given to us.

Our faith determines the level of victory in which we walk. That means we must live with the consciousness that we are a victor in Christ. This requires a victorious "mindset." Afterall, we have been born into a family of overcomers! Believing in Christ Jesus, and his victory, means we can overcome the world (see John 16:33).

> Who is he that overcomes the world, but he that believes that Jesus is the son of God? (1 John 5:4)

Jesus has defeated the enemy, and we are to enforce that victory. But victories only come about in battle. I often say, the bigger the battle, the bigger the victory. Following are great verses to mediate on as you contemplate victory or prepare for the next battle:

> For in him dwelleth all the fulness of the Godhead bodily, and ye are complete in him, which is the head of all principality and power: in whom also ye are circumcised with the circumcision made without hands, in putting off the body of the sins of the

flesh by the circumcision of Christ: buried with him in baptism, wherein also ye are risen with him through the faith of the operation of God, who hath raised him from the dead. You, being dead in your sins and the uncircumcision of your flesh, hath he quickened together with him, having forgiven you all trespasses; Blotting out the handwriting of ordinances that was against us, which was contrary to us, and took it out of the way, nailing it to his cross; and having spoiled principalities and powers, he made a shew of them openly, triumphing over them in it. (Col 2:9-15 KJV)

In Jesus triumph, we have been redeemed! How awesome that we are made to sit with Him in heavenly places. His victory is our victory!

Jesus gained the victory for us, in us, and Jesus is winning victories through us if we will maintain a winning attitude!

If victory in any area belongs to us, what should our response be? We act like a winner!

Victory is an attitude, a confidence that we walk in because we know the victory is ours. We are not trying to get victory. It is ours because of what Jesus has done. His work is finished. The same victories we see in the scriptures can be ours today because we have The Greater One on the inside:

> You are from God, little children, and have overcome them; because greater is He who is in you than he who is in the world. (1 John 4:4)

If the Greater One is on the inside of us, then that means the lesser one is on the outside.

We have victory over death because we have life, victory over lack because we have abundance, over storms because we have peace, over blindness because we have light, over the Goliaths of life because we have the God of life, over the fiery furnaces of life because we have the fire of the

Spirit, over the floods because our God is the standard, over the armies of hell because our Lord has defeated them, over the Red Sea's and the walls of life because we can run through a troop and leap over a wall. We have victory over all. **We fight all our battles from a place of victory seated far above the enemy**.

God's formula for success is still the same, do not be afraid or dismayed just because trouble appears. Jesus left us peace in all circumstances of life:

> I have spoken to you, so that in Me you may have peace. In the world you have tribulation, but take courage; I have overcome the world." (John 16:33)

That is why the Apostle Paul writing to the Corinthians said, "For we walk by faith and not by sight" (2 Corinthians 5:7).

Faith gives us the courage we need to be strong and smile because we already know the outcome. We win! But conversely, doubt will despair, complain and be sad, but **the**

attitude of faith will rejoice, give thanks, and be glad.

By faith, victory is possessed with knowledge and gratitude. Just as the Romans held grand triumphs, which were parades in which they staged idol worship, food, and festivities as they led their captives into Rome, we can see how God in Christ parades us as victors:

> But thanks be to God, Who in Christ always leads us in triumph [as trophies of Christ's victory] and through us spreads and makes evident the fragrance of the knowledge of God everywhere. (2 Corinthians 2:14)

We always triumph in Christ. Confess it daily! That will put a winning attitude in you. **If we always triumph, that means we never fail!**

We never accept defeat as a final verdict, no matter what it looks like or how we feel. That is why we hold fast the confession of our faith. We stand on the Word, and the Word will put us over.

Notice, it is God that causes us to triumph! I can almost hear Paul shouting as he writes to the Corinthians, telling them, "...death is swallowed up in victory" (1 Corinthians 15:54).

The Greek word "Nikos" for triumph means: Victory; A conquest. The Greek word "Nikao" and "Nike," **Victory** means; to subdue, conquer, overcome, prevail, the means of success. **In victory, God wants to use us to perfume the earth with His knowledge.** As we walk in our victory and know Him, we manifest Him. As we accomplish this our victory becomes very attractive to people in need.

God is for you, He is in you, He is leading you, He is behind you, He is beside you, and because you have joined yourself to Him, He will take up your cause. The book of Romans gives us such a voice of victory:

> If God be for us, who can be against us? He that spared not his own Son, but delivered him up for us all, how shall he not with him also freely give us all

things? Who shall lay anything to the charge of God's elect? It is God that justifies. (Romans 8:31-33)

These verses means that you are invincible. **You are unbeatable**. There is no foe that is a match for God. Who can rise up against Almighty God? "But in all these things we overwhelmingly conquer through Him who loved us" (Romans 8:37). Our position of being more than a conqueror is real now!

To conquer means: to triumph, to overcome, to win, to succeed, or to be victorious. To be a conqueror means that you are living the victory kind of life. Living a life of victory can become a way of life.

We need to be so full of the Word we have a strong vision of victory. A well-known hero of inspiring sermons made a wonderful statement: "Half our fears arise from neglect of the Bible" (Spurgeon, Charles, Internet Quote). **Stay full of the Word, and you will stay full of victory**, and less in fear of whatever faces you.

Victory in life is not achieved by formula. Victory comes from knowing God, who you are in Him, and walking by faith. This will require you to say something:

> And they overcame him by the blood of the Lamb, and by the word of their testimony; and they loved not their lives unto the death. (Revelation 12:11)

We believers have absolutely no reason to be intimidated by evil. We have died with Christ. Christ is now living in us, and God has given us two things in this scripture with which to overcome the Devil and intimidation: The blood of the lamb and the word of your testimony! The next chapter on faith will give you encouragement to help you with your reign over the enemy.

Our faith determines the level of victory in which we walk...

To find and to be in God's specific will for your life is to become invincible...

Overcoming in life will require an attitude of faith...

ಖ 5 ಜ

UNDERSTANDING HOW FAITH WORKS

~~~~

Very early one morning, I heard the Holy Spirit speak a phrase to me that I then used to preach a series of messages on faith. I believe the message was life-changing for many. I believe the Lord was emphasizing that we must major on faith. I always say, when the Holy Spirit speaks to you, you always remember where you were and what you were doing as though in a picture. The Holy Spirit wrote this on my heart:

Understanding how faith works is the most important thing. We must become proficient in the use of that which should be normal for the believer.

FAITH IS YOUR DEFENSE AGAINST THE ENEMY

The New Testament is full of warfare references; the weapons of our warfare, the armor of God, a good soldier, fight the good fight, we wrestle, war a good warfare with prophecies spoken over you, our defense, our adversary, etc. and many more. **It seems that the New Testament is a soldier's book**. The earth is certainly a combat zone for the believer, and we are going to have to be people of resistance. 'The Resistance' was the name applied to people who fought against an invading occupation force such as the 'underground' French movement in World War II. We are people of the resistance against a force within—our old nature that tries to rise again, and an outside demonic force. The Apostle Peter warned:

> Be of sober spirit, be on the alert. Your adversary, the devil, prowls around like a roaring lion, seeking someone to devour. But resist him, firm in your faith, knowing that the same experiences of suffering are being

accomplished by your brethren who are in the world. (1 Peter 5:8)

James, the Lord's brother, uses the same terminology concerning our adversary; "Submit therefore to God. Resist the devil and he will flee from you" (James 4:7).

To 'flee' means the devil will run as if in terror. We have the ability to resist the enemy's fiery darts only because we are living a consecrated life, one submitted to God. We need to fully know what it means to resist. What do we do? How do we resist? The apostle Paul gives us insight in his letters. First of all, writing to the Corinthian Church, he said, "Be on the alert, stand firm in the faith, act like men, be strong (1 Corinthians 16:13).

Paul uses this phrase again in his second letter, "in your faith you are standing firm" (2 Corinthians 1:24). **It is obvious that faith is not passive**. Rather, faith is a servant that is accomplishing something! Faith is what gives us a firm stance to resist the enemy, to hold our ground or possess what is ours.   Sometimes   that   takes   standing, standing, and then standing.

Notice the connection Paul makes to the Ephesians concerning resisting and standing:

> Finally, be strong in the Lord and in the strength of His might. Put on the full armor of God, so that you will be able to stand firm against the schemes of the devil. For our struggle is not against flesh and blood, but against the rulers, against the powers, against the world forces of this darkness, against the spiritual forces of wickedness in the heavenly places. Therefore, take up the full armor of God, so that you will be able to resist in the evil day, and having done everything, to stand firm. Stand firm therefore…" (Ephesians 6:10-14)

Paul compares a Roman soldier's gear to God's armor that is available for us in spiritual warfare. The piece of armor we want to focus on is the 'shield of faith.' This is what we use to resist the enemy:

In addition to all, taking up the shield of faith with which you will be able to extinguish all the flaming missiles of the evil one. (Ephesians 6:16)

In every battle, take faith as your wrap-around shield, for it is able to extinguish the blazing arrows coming at you from the Evil One! (Ephesians 6:16, The Passion Translation (TPT)).

The majority of those flaming missiles are going to be thoughts that the enemy sends your way in the middle of circumstances, trials, or difficulties of life that come your way. He is a liar and 'the father of lies,' and is always trying to create doubt, fear and confusion in our lives.

Paul uses the word 'schemes' of the devil which means that the devil has one main method of operation. He uses the same road or tactic as always; He is after your mind and is a master at 'mind games.'

Paul was very clear in his instructions about knowing how our enemy the devil operates, "that no advantage would be taken of us by

Satan, for we are not ignorant of his schemes" (2 Corinthians 2:11).

That is why Paul urged the Corinthian Church:

> Though we walk in the flesh, we do not war according to the flesh, for the weapons of our warfare are not of the flesh, but divinely powerful for the destruction of fortresses. We are destroying speculations and every lofty thing raised up against the knowledge of God, and we are taking every thought captive to the obedience of Christ. (Corinthians 10:3-5)

The first key to resistance is knowing what the Word says so we can destroy strongholds and speculations, and take thoughts captive. The devil delights in filling people's emotions and senses with illusions that captivate their minds and ultimately destroy them. Founder of Rhema Bible Training Center, Kenneth E. Hagin (referred to as Brother Hagin), often compared wrong thoughts (either our own or the enemy's) to birds that fly over our heads, but we do not have to let them build a nest there.

Our faith is the shield of protection. In warfare if something is coming at you, the shield is used as a defense. **Battle is not always our choice but winning is our choice**. That is why we call it a faith fight, and a fight we win. If you have not been in a good faith fight lately, then you should be preparing for one.

God expects us to continually grow in our faith walk. You can compare it to enlarging your faith shield! Since we use the shield in confrontation, that means when a missile of the enemy is fired at us, we respond with the Word of God. If you are on the front lines in ministry, whether five-fold ministry, an intercessor, or a committed believer, it is combat, and you are going to have shots fired your way. We have to learn to lift up the Shield of Faith, and learn to shoot back using God's Word, the Sword of the Spirit. It is the only offensive spiritual piece of armor.

The two best applications of this are shown in the lives of Jesus and Joshua. During His wilderness temptation in which Jesus fasted for forty days, Satan comes at Jesus with three different temptations. Jesus gives us the proper illustration of how to resist, stand, lift up the Shield of Faith, and then use the Sword of the Spirit by quoting Scripture preceded by saying, "It is written".

The instructions that God gave to Joshua are very important for us to understand concerning developing our shield. God instructed him three different times in the first chapter to, "Be strong and of good courage."

God speaks 'the how to'—the gamechanger:

> This book of the law shall not depart from your mouth, but you shall meditate on it day and night, so that you may be careful to do according to all that is written in it; for then you will make your way prosperous, and then you will have success. (Joshua 1:8)

God told Joshua the key to leading the people and being successful was to keep the word in his mouth and meditate. Meditation is not a mental exercise. To meditate means to mutter. We are to mutter the word at all times so it gets down on the inside of us. When the word gets in us our shield begins to develop. Once mediation leads to a heart full of the Word, it becomes a heart full of faith! Jesus said,

> The good man out of the good treasure of his heart brings forth what is good; and the evil man out of the evil treasure brings forth what is evil; for his mouth speaks from that which fills his heart. (Luke 6:45)

A heart full of faith means that we have a developed a good shield to defend us. I can always tell who has their Shield of Faith in place by the smile on their face. If your faith shield is up, then you are smiling!

The day that Brother Keith Moore asked me, "Who is your source," I responded with a smile. This illustrates that you cannot be depressed, sad, and in faith at the same time. If your Faith Shield is strong, then you will have a good smile on your face because you are expecting full victory! The devil needs to know you are a tough warrior! How will he know? Because you laugh a lot.

Believers need warfare tenacity. When under attack, feeling the missiles flying, we need to get in the proverbial 'prayer closet' and fight back. We cannot advance if we are in a 'just quit mode.' Remembering that we have authority, when we stand and speak into the spiritual realm, the Devil runs as if in terror.

Jesus made if very clear that believers have authority over the enemy. Using authority in light of the will of God is vital for every believer to understand.

> Verily I say unto you, Whatsoever ye shall bind on earth shall be bound in heaven: and whatsoever ye shall loose on earth shall be loosed in heaven. (Matthew 18:18)

Faith is not just something we possess, it is to be used! This is why it is important to know who we are in Christ and understand our authority in Christ. **Authority must be exercised, and it is done in faith with boldness**. Take your place and boldly defend yourself with the Shield of Faith and then swing your sword like a bold warrior.

Your sword will only be as effective as your shield—the Word that you have put in your heart for your shield is the same Word that will be used as a sword. When you are fully alert and ready for battle, you are dressed in the full armor of God and ready for battle.

Understanding how faith works is the most important thing. We must become proficient in the use of that which should be normal for the believer...

Be strong in the Lord and in the strength of His might...

Your sword will only be as good as your shield...

೫ 6ಙ

FAITH IS A TOOL

~~~~~

Faith is your tool for accessing all that God has provided. A mighty man of God who had many documented cases in which he raised people from the dead compares faith to a way:

> There is only one way to all the treasures of God, and that is the way of faith. (Wigglesworth, Smith, Internet Quote)

Faith gives us the ability and brings us to a place where we say amen to all that God has said that we can have and do. You will never move forward in life until you get 'the amen' deep within you.

For as many as are the promises of God, in Him they are yes; Therefore also through Him is our Amen to the glory of God through us. (2 Corinthians 1:20)

Did not Jesus say, "All things are possible to him who believes" (Mark 9:23)? 'All things' possible would surely include the promises of God.

No matter what you may be called to do or need in life, it will require faith to accomplish it or obtain it. **Then to fulfill God's plan for your life, you will need the supernatural tool of faith**. God has already made arrangements for us to succeed in life, but it will require faith to follow His plan and to obtain what is needed. Paul wrote the Ephesian Church,

For we are God's [own] handiwork (His workmanship), recreated in Christ Jesus, [born anew] that we may do those good works which God predestined (planned beforehand) for us [taking paths which He prepared ahead of time], that we should walk in them [living the good life which He prearranged and made ready for us to live] (Ephesians 2:10 AMP).

We have example after example in the book of Hebrews that reveal how the hall of faith men and women of God accomplished that for which they are known. We read in the Word that "by faith men of old gained approval "(Heb.11:2).

By faith Abel offered to God a better sacrifice than Cain. By faith Enoch was taken up so that he would not see death. By faith Noah, being warned by God about things not yet seen, in reverence prepared an ark for the salvation of his household. By faith Abraham, when he was called, obeyed by going out to a place which he was to receive for an inheritance. (Hebrews 11:4-80

In all these examples and throughout the Word of God, people who accomplished acts that pleased God, did it with the tool of faith.

In your personal pursuit of God's plan for your life, always remember, it is impossible to separate faith from being led by the Spirit. You will not see the whole plan, so you must walk it out and the Holy Spirit will direct your steps (see Prov. 3:5).

God's plan for your life will require accessing everything you need to fulfill that plan. Peter makes this clear, God has provided everything we need pertaining to life and Godliness (see 2 Peter 1:3).

If you need forgiveness, healing, financial provision, wisdom, grace, and mercy— whatever it might be, faith is the tool for accessing your inheritance. In order to approach the throne of grace we are told, it requires boldness/confidence (see Heb. 4:16)

One of my favorite verses in the New Testament concerning the Word of God is when Paul was closing out his minister's conference in Ephesus where he had called all the leaders together. One of his last admonitions was concerning the Word of God and its power and ability.

And now I commend you to God and to the word of His grace, which is able to build you up and to give you the inheritance among all those who are sanctified. (Acts 20:32)

Notice that last phrase, "give you the inheritance." Anything good and beneficial or what we would call 'your inheritance' has been included in the grace of God. Your inheritance includes 'all the promises,' or the 'all things' pertaining to life and godliness. God has not left anything out that is good.

Faith is our "Amen" and becomes the instrument you need to obtain your inheritance. Remember, "Faith comes by hearing and hearing the Word of God (Romans 10:17). Once heard, the Word must be used in all areas. This is true of initial salvation as well. Writes Paul, "For by grace you have been saved through faith; and that not of yourselves, it is the gift of God" (Ephesians 2:8).

The word saved is the Greek word 'Sozo' which means saved, healed, delivered, set free and made whole. Therefore, by grace you are saved, healed, delivered, set free and made whole through faith. The word 'through' in the Greek language is the word 'dia' which means 'instrument.' Just like a trumpet player uses his instrument to make music, we use the instrument of faith to receive all that has been provided in Christ.

Faith is your tool to accomplish God's plan. But You must put it to work.

The writer of Hebrews explains how we obtain the promises, "Be imitators of those who through faith and patience inherit the promises" (Hebrews 6:12). We could say, through the instrumentation of faith and patience we receive the promises. Even if we did not have anyone else to imitate, we could study and imitate the life of Abraham, and follow in his steps to obtain the promises, just like he did (See Romans 4:12-13).

Notice the connection Paul makes between the promises, faith, and grace:

> For this reason it is by faith, in order that it may be in accordance with grace, so that the promise will be guaranteed

to all the descendants, not only to those who are of the Law, but also to those who are of the faith of Abraham, who is the father of us all. (Romans 4:16)

Abraham, the Father of Faith, is our father if we walk in the same steps in which he walked.

Grace includes everything you need, your promises, all things, and we access all of it by or with the tool of faith.

Therefore, having been justified by faith, we have peace with God through our Lord Jesus Christ, through whom also we have access by faith into this grace in which we stand, and rejoice in hope of the glory of God. (Romans 5:1-2)

God provides the ability, and the provision. We access it with faith just like we would purchase an airline ticket to get on a plane. The plane is the ability (the grace) to get you where you need to go. The ticket is your faith that gets you on board. When you find your seat you can sit down, relax and wait on the peanuts because faith is a rest:

> Therefore, let us fear if, while a promise remains of entering His rest, any one of you may seem to have come short of it. For indeed we have had good news preached to us, just as they also; but the word they heard did not profit them, because it was not united by faith in those who heard. For we who have believed enter that rest... (Hebrews 4:1-3)

How can we rest? Because by the grace of God 'the promises,' 'the all things,' has already been provided. Now we can either use the tool of faith to receive and rest, or imitate the opposite example of disobedience and unbelief as the children of Israel when God brought them out of Egypt to the promised land. They faced their destiny and saw difficulty instead of God's promises.

For no matter how many promises God has made, they are "Yes" in Christ. And so through him the "Amen" is spoken by us to the glory of God. (2 Corinthians 1:20 NIV)

Faith is your tool to accomplish God's plan, but you must put it to work

It is impossible to separate faith from being led by the Spirit

There is only one way to all the treasures of God, and that is the way of faith. (Wigglesworth, Smith, internet quote)

ಜಾ 7 ಐ

FAITH HAS A SHOUT, A LAUGH, A DANCE, AND A RUN!

~~~~~

Some of the most difficult times to shout, laugh, dance, and rejoice are when you are going through a season of testing, trials, and challenges. But God's word tells us how to pass the test with a shout of joy, "Oh, clap your hands, all you peoples! Shout to God with the voice of triumph!" (Psalm 47:1). The NLT says, "shout to God with Joyful praise!"

A good reminder comes from Brother Keith Moore, "Doubt despairs complains and is sad, but faith rejoices, gives thanks and is glad." I heard him say this phrase many times while he was an instructor at Rhema.

James, the brother of Jesus and Pastor of the Church in Jerusalem, begins his letter with faith instructions,

Consider it (count it) all joy, my brethren, when you encounter various trials, knowing that the testing of your faith produces endurance. (James 1:2-3)

Peter has a similar injunction,

In this you greatly rejoice, even though now for a little while, if necessary, you have been distressed by various trials, so that the proof of your faith, being more precious than gold which is perishable, even though tested by fire, may be found to result in praise and glory and honor at the revelation of Jesus Christ; and though you have not seen Him, you love Him, and though you do not see Him now, but believe in Him, you greatly rejoice with joy inexpressible and full of glory, obtaining as the outcome of your faith the salvation of your souls. (1 Peter 1:6-9)

No matter what your situation looks like, faith learns to rejoice, laugh, dance and possibly run because you trust God.

Eliphaz, one of Job's friends said, "At destruction and famine you shall laugh" (Job 5:22).

When your faith is being tested, you need to know that your shout of victory carries a mighty sound with it. Certain verses are worth committing to memory in several translations:

> The sound of joyful shouting and salvation is in the tents of the righteous. (Psalm 118:15)

> Shouts of joy and victory resound in the tents of the righteous: "The Lord's right hand has done mighty things! (Psalm 118:15 NIV)

> My loud shouts of victory will echo throughout the land. (Psalm 118:15 TPT)

> Hear the shouts, hear the triumph songs in the camp of the saved? "The hand of God has turned the tide! (Psalm 118:15 MSG)

Were we to pull up to your house, we should be able to hear some "Hallelujahs," "glory to God", "we are the redeemed," and "Jesus is Lord," going on. (See Psalm 118:15)

When people tell you to be quiet—you are being a little too loud, you just have to learn to get a little bit louder. Most people know the story of Blind Bartimaeus. As Jesus was approaching Jericho, he began crying out with a loud voice, "Jesus, Son of David, have mercy on me!" The crowd kept telling him to be quiet, but he cried out even more. Jesus stopped and had him brought to him and the man ended up being healed. Jesus told him, "Your faith has made you well." His faith started with a shout! (see Mark 10:46-52).

The story of Joshua and the people of God marching around the walls of Jericho for seven days is a popular one. It was their first battle to take the land that God had promised. God instructed them on the last day to march around the walls seven times, and after the seventh time, to shout. And when they did the walls came tumbling down. **Faith for possession started with a shout!** (see Joshua 6).

Faith has a shout to it. That means we shout with boldness right in the face of symptoms, feelings, circumstances and the Devil. You have to learn to take your victory! Smith Wigglesworth was a good example of a life of faith and power. He said, "Many people would be giants in the power of God but they have no shout of faith." (Wigglesworth, Smith Internet Quote). He also said, "No man can doubt if he learns to shout."

When you shout with faith, the spirit realm hears it. A shout of faith also does something inside you. Remember the commercial, "For those tough stains, Shout them out." Compare those stains to problems, and shout them out. The devil is a liar, and your voice needs to get louder than his when he starts talking. You just shout in his face, and declare, "I have the victory." That is called a shout of victory.

There are times in life when you do not just declare it, you must shout about it. Shout to testify of your faith in God's promise. Shout in thankfulness for His glorious mercy. Shout to encourage yourselves and your brethren.

Shout to strike terror into your enemies. (Wesley, John, Internet Quote)

If you believe the Word of God, then you need to shout about it. If you believe God is rich in mercy, then you shout about it. **Never let anyone do your shouting for you**. You must learn to do your own shouting!

If people can shout at a sporting event, surely, we can shout if God is on our side. It is okay to shout in Church—decently and in order of course.

Balaam was a prophet whom Balak, King of the Moabites, wanted to use to bring a curse upon the Israelites. As they both stood on a hill overlooking Israel's camp, Balaam tried several times, and each time the LORD turned the curse into a blessing. Balaam finally told Balak (in my words) "I cannot curse what God has blessed. And by the way, when I see the people, the Lord God is with them, and the shout of a king is among them" (see Numbers 23). Balaam said to Balak,

> God is not a man, that He should lie,
> Nor a son of man, that He should

repent; Has He said, and will He not do it? Or has He spoken, and will He not make it good?" (Numbers 23:19)

We can shout about God's faithfulness to his Word, His promises.

Balaam also said, "I see the people rising up like a lioness and like a lion it lifts itself" (Numbers 23:24). When you are royalty there needs to be the shout of king in the middle of your camp. We are not just talking about any king but the 'King of Kings and the 'Lord of Lords.'

The lion has a roar, and Jesus is the Lion of the tribe of Judah. He is the King of Kings, and He will descend from heaven with a shout (see 1 Thessalonians 4:16).

Churches that lose their shout, lose their ability to influence and affect their generation. Churches sometimes need a corporate shout!

This world is full of demons, principalities, powers, and rulers of this world's darkness. We are instructed in the Word to say something. Using our armor, and using the Sword of the Spirit will mean you are speaking the Word. Often the Scriptures will require speaking,

> Let the redeemed of the Lord say so, Whom He has redeemed from the hand of the adversary (Psalm 107:2).

But don't just say it, shout about it! In Chapter Five where James said, "Submit to God, resist the devil and he will flee in terror," we are not going to resist him with a whisper. No army runs into battle with a whisper. They run into battle with a shout! We shout because we have already won. And winning should produce even more praise and rejoicing instead of fear of failure:

> Weak faith is found in worry, misery, anxiety, little hope, and whining, a soul darkened from its own light. Great faith is found in prayer, gratitude, praise and joy and peace. It presents a face aglow with the Son's shining. (Anonymous)

Demons are afraid of you! God lives in you. They know they are defeated, but they hope that you never find out. When you find out who you are and what you have, and then choose to believe God, something begins to rise inside of you—a shout. No matter what comes your way.

Remember, when you know who you are, you will believe what you say.

Faith has a shout to it ...

The sound of joyful shouting and salvation is in the tents of the righteous. (Psalm 118:15)

"Many people would be giants in the power of God but they have no shout of faith." (Wigglesworth, Smith internet quote)

ASSURANCE OF YOUR SALVATION

If you have any doubts as to your eternal home, or lack assurance that you have perfect peace with God, then pray this prayer out loud from your heart:

"Father, your Word says in **Romans 10:9** that if you confess with your mouth Jesus as Lord, and believe in your heart that God raised Jesus from the dead, you shall be saved. I believe Jesus is Lord, I believe that you raised Him from the dead. I believe that I now receive eternal life through Jesus, according to **John 3:16**. I ask You to forgive me of all my sins, and I receive freedom through the blood of Jesus, according to **Ephesians 1:7**. I thank You that I do not come into judgment, but I have passed out of death and into life, according to **John 5:24**. I ask you to confirm supernatural love, joy, and peace in my life. In Jesus name, Amen."

If you prayed this prayer and made a decision to receive Jesus Christ as your Savior. We would love to hear from you and share in your experience and send you some important information about your next steps.

Email us at info@Brackenchristianministries.org

NOTES

ABOUT THE AUTHOR

Bracken Christian is currently Senior Pastor of Harvest Church in Lubbock, Texas, a Church he pioneered in 1992. While serving as a youth minister in 1988, the Holy Spirit spoke to Bracken that He would use him all over the world. That apostolic call led Bracken to pioneer three affiliate Churches in the West Texas area and travel to the nations.

Bracken now continues that call, travelling domestically and internationally to inspire excellence, vision and the spirit of faith. He made over 50 international trips and has ministered in over 26 Nations and many of those nations frequently.

Bracken is the author of three books with translations in three foreign languages— *Three Kinds of Incense, The Incense of Prayer, and Faith Keys.*

He attended Texas Tech university, is a graduate of Rhema Bible College, and also holds a Master of Arts and Doctor of Ministry in Theology from the International College of Excellence, an affiliate of Life Christian University.

Prior to his education at Rhema and establishing Harvest Church, he served in several churches as Youth Minister, Associate Minister and Worship Pastor. God has gifted him with a heart of worship. This year, Bracken is celebrating 37 years in ministry. Bracken and his wife Donna have four children and three grandchildren.

Cover design: Coley Ambrose
Coleyambrose@gmail.com
Photography: Laure Clark Photography

Other Titles By Dr. Bracken Christian

Visit https://brackenchristianministries.org To Order

Faith Keys
Paperback
Devotional

Faith Keys
Paperback
Devotional
* Spanish

Faith Keys
Paperback
Devotional
* Albanian

**3 Kinds of
Incense**
Paperback Book

**3 Kinds of
Incense**
Paperback Book
* Spanish

24/7 Faith
USB

**Your Race To
Destiny**
USB

**The Core Of
Life**
USB

Other Titles By Dr. Bracken Christian

Visit https://brackenchristianministries.org To Order

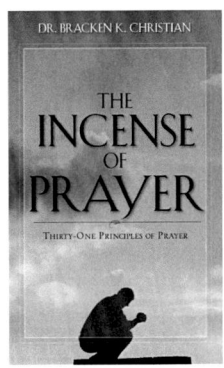

Incense Of Prayer
Paperback Book

Incense Of Prayer
Paperback Book
* Spanish

Incense Of Prayer
Paperback Book
* Albanian

The Fragrance Of Excellence
USB

Overcoming Fear
USB

God's Extravagant Love
USB

The Box
USB

Stretch Your Faith
USB